Parent Training
for Disruptive Behavior

 ✓ PROGRAMS THATWORK

Editors-In-Chief

Anne Marie Albano, PhD

David H. Barlow, PhD

Scientific Advisory Board

Gillian Butler, PhD

David M. Clark, PhD

Edna B. Foa, PhD

Paul J. Frick, PhD

Jack M. Gorman, MD

Kirk Heilbrun, PhD

Robert J. McMahon, PhD

Peter E. Nathan, PhD

Christine Maguth Nezu, PhD

Matthew K. Nock, PhD

Paul Salkovskis, PhD

Bonnie Spring, PhD

Gail Steketee, PhD

John R. Weisz, PhD

G. Terence Wilson, PhD

Parent Training for Disruptive Behavior

The RUBI Autism Network

PARENT WORKBOOK

KAREN BEARSS
CYNTHIA R. JOHNSON
BENJAMIN L. HANDEN
ERIC BUTTER
LUC LECAVALIER
TRISTRAM SMITH
LAWRENCE SCAHILL

OXFORD
UNIVERSITY PRESS

OXFORD
UNIVERSITY PRESS

Oxford University Press is a department of the University of Oxford. It furthers
the University's objective of excellence in research, scholarship, and education
by publishing worldwide. Oxford is a registered trade mark of Oxford University
Press in the UK and certain other countries.

Published in the United States of America by Oxford University Press
198 Madison Avenue, New York, NY 10016, United States of America.

© Oxford University Press 2018

All rights reserved. No part of this publication may be reproduced, stored in
a retrieval system, or transmitted, in any form or by any means, without the
prior permission in writing of Oxford University Press, or as expressly permitted
by law, by license, or under terms agreed with the appropriate reproduction
rights organization. Inquiries concerning reproduction outside the scope of the
above should be sent to the Rights Department, Oxford University Press, at the
address above.

You must not circulate this work in any other form
and you must impose this same condition on any acquirer.

CIP data is on file at the Library of Congress
ISBN 978–0–19–062784–3

15

Printed by Marquis, Canada

One of the most difficult problems for patients with various disorders and diseases is finding the best help available. Everyone is aware of friends or family members who have sought treatment from a seemingly reputable practitioner, only to find out later from another doctor that the original diagnosis was wrong or the treatments recommended were inappropriate or perhaps even harmful. Most patients, or family members, address this problem by reading everything they can about their symptoms, seeking out information on the Internet, or aggressively "asking around" to tap knowledge from friends and acquaintances. Governments and healthcare policymakers are also aware that people in need don't always get the best treatments—something they refer to as "variability in healthcare practices."

Now healthcare systems around the world are attempting to correct this variability by introducing "evidence-based practice." This simply means that it is in everyone's interest that patients get the most up-to-date and effective care for a particular problem. Healthcare policymakers have also recognized that it is very useful to give consumers of healthcare as much information as possible, so that they can make intelligent decisions in a collaborative effort to improve health and mental health. This series, "Programs *ThatWork*," is designed to accomplish just that. Only the latest and most effective interventions for particular problems are described in user-friendly language. To be included in this series, each treatment program must pass the highest standards of evidence available, as determined by a scientific advisory board. Thus, when individuals suffering from these problems or their family members seek out an expert clinician who is familiar with these interventions and decides that they are appropriate, they will have confidence that they are receiving the best care available. Of course, only your healthcare professional can decide on the right mix of treatments for you.

This particular program is designed to teach parents of children with autism spectrum disorder (ASD) how to reduce disruptive behaviors such as aggression, tantrums, noncompliance, and self-injury. As many as half of children with ASD display such behaviors, and many parents struggle with the significant impact such behaviors can have on their child's well-being and family functioning. This approach uses a technique known as parent training (PT), which has been used extensively to reduce problematic behaviors in children without ASD from preschool age through adolescence, and recent research supports the implementation of PT with children with ASD. By undertaking this program with the support of a skilled clinician, parents can help reduce their children's most difficult behaviors, leading to more harmonious homes and healthier, happier families.

Anne Marie Albano, Editor-in-Chief
David H. Barlow, Editor-in-Chief
Programs *That Work*

Contents

Acknowledgments

Many thanks to our colleagues, Michael Aman, L. Eugene Arnold, Christopher McDougle, Jim Mulick, Denis Sukhodolsky, Noha Minshawi, Naomi Swiezy, and Susan White, for their contributions to the development of this manual.

Welcome to the RUBI Parent Workbook! This program is designed to help you learn strategies designed to reduce your child's problem behaviors, such as tantrums, noncompliance, aggression, and self-injurious behaviors, as well as improve daily living skills, such as getting dressed, bathing, and brushing teeth. Topics include the following:

- How to prevent problem behaviors from happening in the first place
- How to follow a daily routine that will increase predictability in your child's schedule
- How to reinforce the appropriate behavior you hope to see more of
- How to respond when problem behavior occurs
- How to teach your child new skills
- How to make sure all the positive change that occurs in your child's behavior over the course of the program continues over time and extends to different people and situations

The RUBI Parent Training program is composed of 11 sessions that all families participate in. Your clinician may also decide to conduct a home visit as well as booster sessions once you have completed the program. Lastly, there are some supplemental sessions that you and your clinician can complete in order to help with problems that may require extra attention, such as sleep, feeding, and toileting issues.

Immediately following this introduction, you will find a blank Behavior Support Plan (BSP). This is a document that you will work on with your clinician at every session. Specifically, you will use it to document all of the new strategies you and your clinician come up with each week. The BSP also will be reviewed and revised by you and your clinician during each Parent Training session. Specifically, each session will start with review of the homework from the previous session as well as a review and update of the BSP. The review of the BSP at each session provides an opportunity for you to discuss successes and challenges of previous behavioral strategies. The review can be used to identify problems, refine ongoing interventions, and develop new strategies. These adjustments will then be added to the BSP. Because the BSP builds over time, the completed, final document will provide a rich description of all the different intervention strategies you and your clinician came up with to help address your child's problem behavior and to improve his or her daily living skills.

Next, you will see materials that you will use for each session:

- *In-Session Activity Sheets.* Each session includes worksheets for you to complete with the clinician during sessions.
- *Homework Activity Sheets.* Each session you will be assigned homework to practice the skill you and your clinician have chosen to implement over the week. You are encouraged to use the homework activity sheets to document your progress (successes and challenges!) with implementing the homework. This will help you to problem-solve any issues with your clinician at the next session.
- *Session Review Sheets.* Each session includes a review sheet summarizing the content of the session. You are encouraged to show this material to your child's other caregivers to help support their implementation of strategies that are chosen for homework.

RUBI studies indicate that many children with ASD and their families benefit from the RUBI Parent Training program. Thank you for using this program!

Child's Name: _____   ID _____

Behavior Support Plan

TARGET PROBLEM BEHAVIORS: Definition of the behaviors we want to address in treatment (Topography)	
Behavior 1:	
Behavior 2:	
Behavior 3:	
Behavior 4:	

PERCEIVED FUNCTION(S): The cause of target behaviors	
Behavior 1:	
Behavior 2:	
Behavior 3:	
Behavior 4:	

PREDICTORS/TRIGGERS FOR PROBLEM BEHAVIORS: Situations that may cause the behaviors to occur more frequently

Child's Name: ID

Behavior Support Plan

| DATA COLLECTION: |
| How to track progress of problem behaviors |

Acronym	What It Stands for	Definition	Examples
A	Antecedent	Cue or trigger that occurs right before the behavior takes place	▪ Being told what to do ▪ Not getting what the child wants ▪ Not getting attention
B	Behavior	The target behavior that can be observed, counted, or timed	▪ Hitting ▪ Yelling ▪ Talking back ▪ Whining
C	Consequence	What occurs right after the behavior; can be positive or negative	▪ Time out ▪ Privilege removal ▪ Ignore ▪ Reward ▪ Hug/praise

1) Use your ABC's to determine the function of the behavior:
   ▪ To escape or "get out of doing" demands
   ▪ To get attention
   ▪ To "get what the child wants"
   ▪ Because it's "self-stimulatory"

2) Determine which behavioral strategy (or strategies) would make the most sense to target the *function* of the behavior

3) Create/use data tracking forms to track your implementation of the strategy and progress in terms of changes in the child's behavior

Child's Name: ID

Behavior Support Plan

PREVENTION STRATEGIES (ANTECEDENTS): *What we are going to do so the behaviors do not occur in the first place*		
STRATEGY	**SPECIFIC DETAILS**	**DATE INITIATED**

Child's Name: ID

Behavior Support Plan

REINFORCERS: *Items or activities that are motivating to the child*	
Primary Reinforcers	
Social Reinforcers	
Tangible Reinforcers	
Activities/Privileges	
Token Reinforcers	

Additional Notes About Reinforcers:

Reinforcers work best if:

- Access to the reinforcer is limited **except** in the context of the behavioral contingency
- The child really wants to work for the reinforcer
- The reinforcer is given ONLY when the child successfully completes the behavior

Child's Name: ID

Behavior Support Plan

REINFORCEMENT STRATEGIES: _Ways to provide your child with rewards for good behaviors_		
STRATEGY	**SPECIFIC DETAILS**	**DATE INITIATED**

Child's Name: ID

Behavior Support Plan

	OTHER CONSEQUENCE STRATEGIES: *What to do AFTER the behaviors occur*	
STRATEGY	**SPECIFIC DETAILS**	**DATE INITIATED**

Child's Name: _____   ID

Behavior Support Plan

TEACHING STRATEGIES: What we are going to teach the child so the behaviors do not occur		
STRATEGY	**SPECIFIC DETAILS**	**DATE INITIATED**

Child's Name: ID

Behavior Support Plan

	SUPPLEMENTAL SESSIONS:

Behavior Support Plan

MAINTENANCE/GENERALIZATION:
How to MAINTAIN low rates of problem behavior in all environments

Tips for Maintaining Behaviors:

1. Continued reinforcement is important in maintaining a behavior.

2. Fade reinforcement of the new skill to a more realistic reinforcement schedule.

   One way would be to move from reinforcing a behavior every time to reinforcing a behavior every third or fifth time; this would be an example of **intermittent reinforcement**.

   Another way to provide reinforcement less often is to use **delayed reinforcement**, which means you reinforce a behavior not immediately but after a certain period of time.

Tips for Promoting Generalization of Skills Across Settings and People:

1. New skills are more likely to be generalized if they are reinforced across different settings.

2. It is helpful to use reinforcers that naturally occur in different settings.

3. If a situation is too different from the one the skill was learned in, sometimes the new skill will not generalize to the new situation.

4. Finally, make sure a problematic behavior is not being reinforced in situations outside of the home.

Child's Name: ID

Behavior Support Plan

STRATEGY	SPECIFIC DETAILS

Core Sessions

Activity Sheet 1.1

Session Outline

	Sessions	Skills/Activities
1	Behavioral Principles	Introduce overall treatment goals Introduce concepts of functions of behavior, antecedents, and consequences of behavior
2	Prevention Strategies	Discuss antecedents to behavior problems and develop preventive strategies
3	Daily Schedules	Develop a daily schedule and identify points of intervention (including use of visual schedules) to decrease behavior problems
4	Reinforcement 1	Introduce concept of reinforcers—to promote compliance, strengthen desired behaviors, and teach new behaviors
5	Reinforcement 2	Introduce "catching your child being good" Teach play and social skills through child-led play
6	Planned Ignoring	Explore systematic use of extinction (via planned ignoring) to reduce behavioral problems
7	Compliance Training	Introduce effective parental requests and the use of guided compliance to enhance compliance and manage noncompliant behaviors
8	Functional Communication Training	Through systematic reinforcement, teach alternative communicative skills to replace problematic behaviors

	Sessions	Skills/Activities
9	Teaching Skills 1	Using task analysis and chaining, provide tools to replace problem behaviors with appropriate behaviors and how to promote new adaptive, coping and leisure skills
10	Teaching Skills 2	Teach various prompting procedures to use while teaching skills
11	Generalization and Maintenance	Generate strategies to consolidate positive behavior changes and generalize newly learned skills
	Home Visit[1]	Observe the child in the natural environment Learn about the layout of the child's home Plan implementation of strategies
	Telephone Booster	Review implementation of intervention strategies Develop interventions for any newly emerging behavior concerns

[1] The home visit can be delivered early on or later in treatment, at the clinician's discretion.

	Supplemental Sessions	Skills/Activities
1	Token Economy Systems	This session provides parents with information on the proper use of token economies, star charts, and point systems to promote positive behaviors in the home and community.
2	Feeding Problems	This session helps the parents address a range of feeding problems that are commonly seen in children with ASD, such as food selectivity, mealtime behavior problems, and overeating.
3	Imitation Skills	This session teaches parents fundamental skills for helping their child learn to imitate others.
4	Sleep Problems	This session provides information on how to address bedtime and sleep problems often observed in children with ASD, such as difficulties with bedtime routines, delayed sleep onset, night awakening, sleep association problems, and the child entering the parents' bed.
5	Time Out	This session provides information on the proper use of time out, how to problem-solve if issues arise, and how to develop and implement a time out plan at home.
6	Toilet Training	This session helps the parents address a range of possible toileting issues such as diaper rituals, refusal to use the toilet, and nighttime toileting problems.
7	Crisis Management	This session provides an opportunity to problem-solve the management of dangerous child behaviors, family crises, and pressing educational issues.

Activity Sheet 1.2

The ABC Model

A = Antecedent: What occurs BEFORE, as a "trigger" to, the behavior

B = Behavior: Child's specific response

C = Consequence: What occurs AFTER, and in response to, the behavior

Activity Sheet 1.3

Identifying Antecedents

#1. Susan hits Fred after he takes the book she is looking at.

Antecedent: _____

#2. Mary starts to interrupt her father by screaming when he is talking on the telephone.

Antecedent: _____

#3. Randy throws his vegetables after his mother puts them on his plate.

Antecedent: _____

#4. Noah screams when he sees the playground on the way to the doctor's office.

Antecedent: _____

Activity Sheet 1.4

Mother/Clinician Exchanges

Exchange #1

Mother: "Tom has been disobedient at home. Is he bad during therapy?"

Clinician: "Tom is usually good, but sometimes he is stubborn."

Exchange #2

Mother: "Tom has been hitting me at home. Does he hit you during therapy?"

Clinician: "No, he hasn't hit me, but he has pulled my hair."

Behavioral Definitions: How can these terms be defined behaviorally?

(Rules of thumb: can count or time)

Aggression:

_____

_____

_____

Disruptive:

_____

_____

_____

Activity Sheet 1.5

Identifying the Function of Behaviors

ANTECEDENT
Ryan is given a turkey sandwich for lunch.

BEHAVIOR
Ryan falls to the floor and screams that he want pop tarts for lunch.

CONSEQUENCE
His mother takes the sandwich away and starts toasting some pop tarts.

Possible Function
Escape/Avoidance
Attention-seeking
To Get What He Wants
"Automatically rewarding"

ANTECEDENT
Ryan gets in the car to drive to school.

BEHAVIOR
Ryan starts to flap his hands.

CONSEQUENCE
His mother turns the radio on to his favorite station.

Possible Function
Escape/Avoidance
Attention-seeking
To Get What He Wants
"Automatically rewarding"

ANTECEDENT
Ryan's mother tells him to clean his room.

BEHAVIOR
Ryan cries and whines to his mom that he doesn't want to clean his room now.

CONSEQUENCE
His mother gives him a hug, tells him not to cry, and talks to him about the importance of keeping his room clean.

Possible Function
Escape/Avoidance
Attention-seeking
To Get What He Wants
"Automatically rewarding"

ANTECEDENT
Ryan's mother tells him to do his homework.

BEHAVIOR
Ryan runs away into his bedroom.

CONSEQUENCE
His mother lets him stay up there because he is being quiet.

Possible Function
Escape/Avoidance
Attention-seeking
To Get What He Wants
"Automatically rewarding"

Activity Sheet 1.6

Pulling It All Together:
Identifying Antecedents, Behavior,
Consequences, and Functions of Behavior

#1: Michael is watching cartoons with his brother in the family room when his brother suddenly decides to change the channel. Michael hits his brother, and Michael's mother scolds him and sends him to his room.

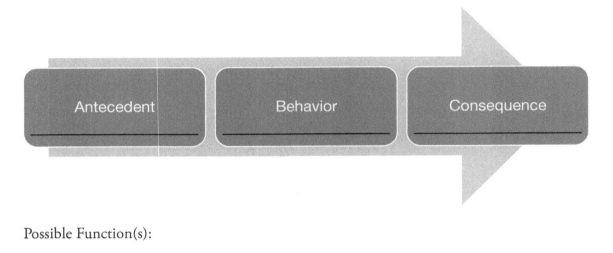

Antecedent ____ Behavior ____ Consequence ____

Possible Function(s):

_____

#2: Susie is playing a game on the computer when her father tells her that it is time to turn it off so she can start her homework. Susie falls to the floor, screaming and kicking. In an attempt to stop Susie from waking up her baby sister from her nap, Susie's father tells her that she can have a few more minutes on the computer.

Antecedent ____ Behavior ____ Consequence ____

Possible Function(s):

_____

Activity Sheet 1.7

ABC (Antecedent-Behavior-Consequence) Data Sheet

Date	Beginning/ Ending Time	Setting	Activity	Who Was Involved	Antecedent: What Happened Right Before the Behavior?	Behavior: What Did It Look Like?	Consequence: What Happened After the Behavior; How Was the Behavior Handled?	Function of the Behavior (Circle Hypothesized Function)
								Escape/avoid Attention To get what child wants Automatically rewarding
								Escape/avoid Attention To get what child wants Automatically rewarding
								Escape/avoid Attention To get what child wants Automatically rewarding
								Escape/avoid Attention To get what child wants Automatically rewarding

Activity Sheet 1.7

ABC (Antecedent-Behavior-Consequence) Data Sheet

Date	Beginning/ Ending Time	Setting	Activity	Who Was Involved	Antecedent: What Happened Right Before the Behavior?	Behavior: What Did It Look Like?	Consequence: What Happened After the Behavior; How Was the Behavior Handled?	Function of the Behavior (Circle Hypothesized Function)
								Escape/avoid Attention To get what child wants Automatically rewarding
								Escape/avoid Attention To get what child wants Automatically rewarding
								Escape/avoid Attention To get what child wants Automatically rewarding
								Escape/avoid Attention To get what child wants Automatically rewarding

Activity Sheet 1.7

ABC (Antecedent-Behavior-Consequence) Data Sheet

Date	Beginning/ Ending Time	Setting	Activity	Who Was Involved	Antecedent: What Happened Right Before the Behavior?	Behavior: What Did It Look Like?	Consequence: What Happened After the Behavior; How Was the Behavior Handled?	Function of the Behavior (Circle Hypothesized Function)
								Escape/avoid Attention To get what child wants Automatically rewarding
								Escape/avoid Attention To get what child wants Automatically rewarding
								Escape/avoid Attention To get what child wants Automatically rewarding
								Escape/avoid Attention To get what child wants Automatically rewarding

Activity Sheet 1.7

ABC (Antecedent-Behavior-Consequence) Data Sheet

Date	Beginning/ Ending Time	Setting	Activity	Who Was Involved	Antecedent: What Happened Right Before the Behavior?	Behavior: What Did It Look Like?	Consequence: What Happened After the Behavior; How Was the Behavior Handled?	Function of the Behavior (Circle Hypothesized Function)
								Escape/avoid Attention To get what child wants Automatically rewarding
								Escape/avoid Attention To get what child wants Automatically rewarding
								Escape/avoid Attention To get what child wants Automatically rewarding
								Escape/avoid Attention To get what child wants Automatically rewarding

Session One Review

What Is an Antecedent? The antecedent is the situation or event that comes before a behavior. It is sometimes described as the "trigger" for the behavior that follows. An antecedent can be an event (telephone ringing, going a different route to school), a person (the music teacher but not the art teacher), or object (stop sign, plate of cookies) in the environment that cues a person to do something.

What Is a Behavior? A central idea of the ABC model is that the majority of behaviors we display are learned. In the ABC model, we are very specific about how we use the term "behavior." A behavior is any action that can be observed and counted or timed. In this model, we want to define behaviors specifically so everyone working with a child will know what specific behavior is occurring.

What Is a Consequence? Consequences describe what happens immediately after, and in response to, a behavior. Some consequences are natural, like getting a ticket for running a red light or getting a Coke after putting money in a vending machine. Others are planned, like giving a time out when a child hits someone. Behaviors are learned over the years by imitating others or by being directly taught. Consequences are what help maintain behaviors; that is, they make it more likely that the behavior will continue. For example, a child learns to raise her hand in school because the teacher calls on her. A child may learn not to hit if the consequence is losing time on the computer.

Functions or Purpose of Disruptive Behaviors: There are a few reasons why a child may be disruptive:

1. The behavior has allowed the child to escape or avoid a situation.
2. The behavior has allowed the child to get attention.
3. The behavior has allowed the child to get what he or she wanted (a toy, the IPad).
4. The behavior is pleasing to the child (for sensory input, "automatically rewarding," relieves anxiety).

Functional Behavior Assessment: By keeping a record of behaviors and their antecedents and consequences, we can better understand the possible function, or purpose, of a particular behavior. We can then make better decisions about how to change the behavior.

Behavior Support Plan: This document summarizes strategies developed for your child through the course of the program. Along with documenting target behaviors and their function, the Behavior Support Plan summarizes three main components of the program: Prevention Strategies, Teaching Alternative Skills, and Consequences.

Activity Sheet 2.1a

Examples of Categories of Prevention Strategies

Avoid situations or people (don't go to movies or house of worship)	We never take our child to the movies. He can't sit that long.
Control the environment (put locks on doors)	We have alarms on our front door, in case our son attempts to leave the house.
Do things in small doses (go shopping for less than an hour)	When we go to my other son's basketball games, my husband takes our son for a walk after being in the gym for 15 minutes.
Change order of events (child must dress before TV)	We used to let the kids watch TV while they eat. But they never seemed to finish, and we kept yelling at them to eat. So now we have a rule: no TV until after dinner.
Respond to early signs of the problem (distract child or change demands)	We can usually tell when our son can no longer sit in a restaurant. As soon as we see him becoming antsy, my husband will take him for a walk.
Change how you ask or respond (don't say "no"; give choices)	With our son, giving choices often lessens noncompliant behavior. For example, before bedtime we offer the choice between two books.
Address setting events (sleep loss, illness, hunger)	School staff reported that our son was becoming more irritable and aggressive between 11 am and noon every day at school. We came up with a plan to give him a small snack around 10:30 am, and the problem has been eliminated.
Use visual or auditory cues (pictures, lists, timers)	Our son used to be cranky during transitions at school. His teacher gave him a picture schedule showing all the activities for the day. She had him check his schedule before each transition.

Activity Sheet 2.1b

Categories of Prevention Strategies

Avoid situations or people (don't go to movies or house of worship)	
Control the environment (put locks on doors)	
Do things in small doses (go shopping for less than an hour)	
Change order of events (child must dress before TV)	
Respond to early signs of the problem (distract child or change demands)	
Change how you ask or respond (don't say "no"; give choices)	
Address setting events (sleep loss, illness, hunger)	
Use visual or auditory cues (pictures, lists, timers)	

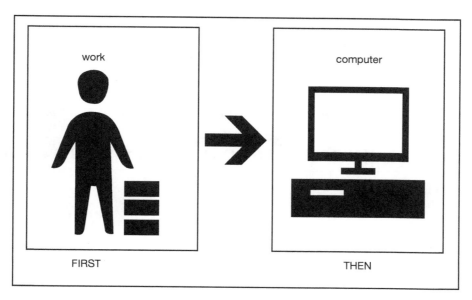

Figure 2.1

Example of a first-then board.

Activity Sheet 2.2

Video Vignettes

Check the box if a strategy from that category can be used to prevent the behavior problem.

CATEGORY	VIDEO #1	VIDEO #2	VIDEO #3	VIDEO #4	VIDEO #5
Avoid situations or people (don't go to movies or house of worship)					
Control the environment (put locks on doors)					
Do things in small doses (go shopping for less than an hour)					
Change order of events (child must dress before TV)					
Respond to early signs of the problem (distract child or change demands)					
Change how you ask or respond (don't say "no"; give choices)					
Address setting events (sleep loss, illness, hunger)					
Use visual or auditory cues (pictures, lists, timers)					

Activity Sheet 2.3a

Example of an Antecedent Management Data Sheet

Date	Time	Target Behavior	Prevention Strategy	How Well Did It Work?			
11/1/20xx	10:15 am	Has tantrums during transitions	Gave 5-minute warning; had child check picture schedule	Had a 10-minute tantrum			
11/2/20xx	08:45 pm	Has tantrums when told to get ready for bed	Gave 5-minute warning; had child check picture schedule	Whined, but no tantrum			
11/3/20xx	8:10 am	Has tantrums when told to put coat on for school	Gave 5-minute warning; had child check picture schedule	Whined, but no tantrum			
11/3/20xx	08:45 pm	Has tantrums when told to get ready for bed	Gave 5-minute warning; had child check picture schedule	Complied; no tantrum or whining			

Activity Sheet 2.3b

Antecedent Management Data Sheet

Date	Time	Target Behavior	Prevention Strategy	How Well Did It Work?

Session Two Review

1. **Avoid Specific Situations or People:** It may be possible to prevent some problem behaviors by limiting trips to restaurants, shops, places of worship, or places that involve waiting in line.

2. **Control the Environment**: Examples include putting locks on cabinets or locking doors from the inside to prevent the child from leaving the house. Some teachers control the classroom environment by seating the child away from others who tend to set the child off or by using partitions that limit distractions.

3. **Do Things in Small Doses or Steps**: A child may be able to handle situations for short periods—but behavior may deteriorate over time. Rather than avoid these situations entirely, parents may instead limit the time spent in certain settings or the number of places they go. For example, families find that multiple errands don't work, but a single trip to the grocery store can be successful.

4. **Change the Order of Events**: When engaged in a preferred activity (e.g., playing with an iPad), some children actively protest when asked to switch gears and comply with a routine demand. The parent can reverse the order and have the child complete the demand before having access to the preferred activity.

5. **Respond to Early Signs of the Problem**: Some parents may notice a "look" in their child's eyes or other signals that the child is becoming more irritated. When this occurs, parents can provide additional assistance so the child can succeed quickly with the demand. Parents may also remove the child from the stressful situation to allow him to calm down.

6. **Change How You Ask or Respond**: We often hear parents say that their child gets agitated when they are told "No." Instead, consider providing choices when making requests, using humor, or giving a child notice that he will need to stop what he's doing in 5 minutes.

7. **Address Setting Events**: Setting events are general conditions or situations that affect the child's behavior. Possible setting events include being tired, hungry, or worried about being separated from a parent. For example, consider a home situation with a radio playing, Xbox humming, and computer whirring. The parent issues a routine request and the child unravels into a meltdown. The routine request could be considered the antecedent, but the setting event (background noise) likely played a role in the child's behavior.

8. **Use Visual or Auditory Cues**: Visual or auditory cues, such as pictures, written lists, or timers, can remind the child about transitions from one activity to another. Visual and auditory cues can help the child process information, provide a sense of predictability, and promote flexibility and independence with the tasks of everyday living. Examples of visual strategies include visual schedules and first-then boards.

Activity Sheet 3.1

Daily Schedule

Time	Activity	Problem Area or Potential Reinforcer	Potential Prevention Strategy

Activity Sheet 3.2

Video Vignettes

Check the box if a strategy from that category can be used to prevent the behavior problem.

CATEGORY	VIDEO #1	VIDEO #2	VIDEO #3	VIDEO #4
Change the time of a demand				
Use fun activities to reward completion of less desired activities				
Establish a routine				
Avoid certain situations or people				
Control the environment				
Do things in small doses				
Change the order of events				
Respond to early signs of problem				
Change how you ask or respond				
Address setting events				
Use visual structure/auditory cues				

Figure 3.1

Daily schedules

Activity Sheet 3.3

Planning the Format of the Visual Schedule

Here are some considerations for the format of your child's visual schedule:

Object	Photo	Icon	Sight Word
Little to no prior experience with visual schedules	Child shows interest in photographs	Child is able to attach meaning to visual presentations other than photographs (e.g., labels on boxes, cartoon images)	Child is at least a beginning reader
Child is a tactile and visual learner	Child can point to or name specific items within the picture		Child is able to attach meaning to the written form of a word
Child is able to or starting to associate meaning with an object or place	Child is able to attach meaning to and/or gain information from photographs	Child can recognize varying visual representations of an object	Child can match a visual representation of an item to the written word form
Pictures and photographs still too abstract; child not able to attach meaning to these visual images	Child is able to match an object to a photo of the same object	Child can group items by at least one attribute	Child operates in a variety of settings where written text is displayed
		Child can match a photo to an icon representing the same item or place	

Activity Sheet 3.4

Visual Schedule Activities

Format of Schedule (CIRCLE):   OBJECT   PHOTO   ICON   WORD/LIST

Scope of Visual Schedule (CIRCLE):   ENTIRE DAY   TARGETED ROUTINE

Initial Number of Items on the Visual Schedule: _____

Location of Visual Schedule: _____

Location of Envelope: ATTACHED TO SCHEDULE   PLACED NEAR SCHEDULE

	Picture Schedule Activity	Comments
1		
2		
3		
4		
5		
6		
7		
8		
9		
10		

Comments: *Note how much guidance the child needed to follow the schedule and any difficulties (child refuses to check schedule, has difficulty getting access to the schedule, tries to change order or get rid of pictures).*

Activity Sheet 3.5

Antecedent Management Data Sheet

Date	Time	Target Behavior	Prevention Strategy	How Well Did It Work?

Session Three Review

Prevention Strategies for Addressing Problems With Your Child's Daily Routine

1. Change the time of a demand.

2. Use fun activities to reward completion of less desired activities.

3. Establish a routine.

Visual Schedules

We know that many children with ASD have difficulty with transitions and unexpected changes in their routines. One way to help children with ASD understand their routines or cope with unexpected changes in their routines is to use a visual schedule.

Visual schedules are often made of selected small icons or pictures that are attached to a board or stable surface with Velcro. The picture or icons can be removed as each successive step is accomplished. The board should be small enough and light enough to carry, but large enough to place the icons in series. The picture schedule highlights the series and sequence of events and activities for the day. It can also be used to direct the child to the next activity. The pictures and symbols provide information that makes the environment appear more stable and predictable, which, in turn, can increase comfort, flexibility, and independence. It often works like this:

1. Place the schedule in a central place.

2. Encourage your child to check the schedule.

3. Review the schedule with the child and select the first picture.

4. Encourage the child to state the activity out loud. For younger or nonverbal children, say it out loud for the child.

5. Have your child take the picture off the schedule and take it with him to the designated area.

6. Complete the activity on the picture.

7. Return to the visual schedule.

8. Have a small box or envelope near the schedule where your child can place the picture of the completed task.

9. Move on to the next picture of the visual schedule.

The visual schedule can be for the entire day. Alternatively, a "mini-schedule" can be created for a selected period—for example, a time of day involving multiple transitions. Visual schedules may take various forms and can be individualized for the child.

Activity Sheet 4.1

Identifying Reinforcers

A.   List six items or activities that might be reinforcing to your child

1 _____

2 _____

3 _____

4 _____

5 _____

6 _____

B.   Primary Reinforcers

1 _____

2 _____

3 _____

4 _____

5 _____

C.   Social Reinforcers

1 _____

2 _____

3 _____

4 _____

5 _____

D. Tangible Reinforcers

    1 _____

    2 _____

    3 _____

    4 _____

    5 _____

E. Activities/Privileges

    1 _____

    2 _____

    3 _____

    4 _____

    5 _____

F. Token Reinforcers

    1 _____

    2 _____

    3 _____

    4 _____

    5 _____

Activity Sheet 4.2

How to Select a Reinforcer

1. What are some unusual activities or preferences your child has that could be used as a reinforcer?

_____

_____

_____

2. What are some natural reinforcers that might be available for your child or other children in your family?

_____

_____

_____

3. What are some privileges that your child currently has free access to that might instead be used contingently?

_____

_____

_____

What would be your Top Five Reinforcers?

1 _____

2 _____

3 _____

4 _____

5 _____

Activity Sheet 4.3

How to Use Reinforcement to Change Behavior

Step 1: Select the target problem behavior to reinforce

Step 2: Keep the behavioral requirement reasonable

Step 3: Decide how often to reinforce behavior

Step 4: Apply reinforcers closely after the behavior

Step 5: Use reinforcers contingently

Step 6: Maintain reinforcer value

Step 7: Pair social and activity/material reinforcement

Step 8: Consider using visual reminders of the desired behavior and reinforcer

Activity Sheet 4.4

Homework Sheet

Behavior #1 _____

Reinforcer: _____

When during the day can you practice reinforcing this behavior? _____

_____

Practice Opportunities	Date	Comments

Behavior #2 _____

Reinforcer: _____

When during the day can you practice reinforcing this behavior? _____

_____

Practice Opportunities	Date	Comments

Session Four Review

Overview of Reinforcement

Reinforcers can be any item, activity, and/or social response (e.g., foods, drinks, toys, activities, attention, and praise) that increase the chance of behavior occurrence. They follow a child's behavior and can be used to strengthen desired behaviors or to help teach new behaviors and skills. Things that are "typically" reinforcing to many children might not be reinforcing to a child with ASD. This may require thinking creatively about what can be a reinforcer for your child.

Five Types of Reinforcers

1. *Primary Reinforcers* typically involve food or drink.
2. *Social Reinforcers* include hugs, high-fives, praise, or any kind of social attention.
3. *Tangible Reinforcers* include enjoyable items such as a favorite toy.
4. *Activities/Privileges* include enjoyable activities such as going to the park, riding bikes, one-on-one time with mom, watching TV, and swimming.
5. *Tokens* are reinforcers that have no value in and of themselves. They gain their value in their ability to "purchase" social, activity, material, and primary reinforcers. Tokens can be points, stars, or even money. The child saves the tokens until he can exchange them for a reinforcer. Tokens are used with children who can wait for a reinforcer and can understand the connection between the token and what they will exchange it for.

You can identify reinforcers for your child by:

- Asking your child what he or she likes
- Talking with others who know the child well, including teachers
- Holding up some reinforcement options and see what the child chooses
- Watching the child to see what he or she does when given free time

How to Select a Reinforcer

- Every child is different and has different likes and dislikes.
- Use natural reinforcers when possible. These are already available in a child's home or school and often have been given "noncontingently," which means they are provided regardless of the child's behavior.
- Make privileges contingent on appropriate behavior. Many children have access to numerous privileges (e.g., TV, computer, time with their friends, favorite toys) despite having behavior problems. Privileges can be used to reinforce desired behavior.
- Reinforcers may change with different developmental periods. Keep in mind your child's developmental level and rapidly changing interests when selecting reinforcers.

Bribery vs. Reinforcement

Some parents feel that using reinforcement to get the child to comply is bribery. Reinforcement and bribery are different concepts, however, with the main difference involving when the reinforcer is being offered. Reinforcers are better applied when the contingency between the behavior and the reinforcer is offered upfront instead of negotiated after the fact. If negotiated after the fact, the child may learn to refuse to comply unless offered something.

Steps when Using Reinforcers to Change Your Child's Behavior

Step 1 Select the target behavior.

Step 2 Keep the behavioral requirement reasonable. This may require that the demand initially be shortened or lessened.

Step 3 It is best to reinforce your child every time. Once behaviors are learned, reinforcers can be gradually faded. Using reinforcement "intermittently," or every once and a while, also can help maintain a new behavior or skill.

Step 4 Be sure that reinforcers are initially given closely following the behavior. If there is too much time between the behavior and the reinforcer (e.g., even several seconds), some children may not understand what behavior is being reinforced.

Step 5 Be sure to use reinforcers contingently. It is like a mini-contract, which means that when the child does the desired behavior, he or she will get the reinforcer.

Step 6 Be sure to maintain reinforcer value. Some reinforcers lose their value because they are given freely in another setting.

Step 7 Be sure to pair social and activity/material reinforcement. Be specific in your praise by letting the child know exactly what you are reinforcing. This helps your child to better understand what behavior is being reinforced.

Step 8 Consider using visual cues of the behavior and reinforcer. This helps to cue the child about the expected behavior, the reinforcer, and the steps needed to earn it.

Contingent reinforcement means providing reinforcement immediately after a positive behavior you wish to see increase and not providing reinforcement after negative or disruptive behaviors that you do not wish to increase.

Activity Sheet 5.1

Ginny constantly fought with her younger sister. Ginny's mother reported that it took twice as long to cook dinner each night because she had to stop and leave the kitchen to yell at Ginny to leave her sister alone. One night last week, one of Ginny's favorite TV programs was on while her mother prepared dinner. Ginny and her sister were as quiet as mice for the entire half-hour program. Ginny's mother was thrilled and remained in the kitchen so as not to disturb the girls.

Activity Sheet 5.2

"Catching Your Child Being Good"

1. What are some behaviors that would be useful to target using the "Catch them while they're good" method?

   _____

   _____

   _____

   _____

2. Do you think your child would respond well to just social reinforcement? _____

   If not, what other types of reinforcers could you use when "Catching your child being good?"

   _____

   _____

   _____

   _____

Activity Sheet 5.3

Play Time

What kinds of toys do you and your child play with together?

_____

_____

_____

_____

How often are you able to play with your child?

_____

_____

_____

_____

How does your child respond to your attempts to join the play?

_____

_____

_____

_____

What difficulties arise when you play with your child (e.g., repetitive play, aggression)?

_____

_____

_____

_____

Activity Sheet 5.4

Play Skills

1) **Spend the first few moments JUST OBSERVING your child. Then,**

2) **IMITATE your child's play.**
   - Focus on what your child is doing. For example, if your child is drawing a tree, start drawing a tree.
   - This shows you are interested in and want to be a part of your child's play.

3) **DESCRIBE your child's behavior.**
   - Provide a running commentary of your child's play.
   - Be descriptive. State exactly what your child is doing: "You're pushing a train around the track."
   - This lets your child know that you're interested and paying attention.
   - You can promote learning by emphasizing certain words (e.g., "You're pushing the red car.")

4) **REFLECT your child's vocalizations.**
   - Repeat or paraphrase what your child says.
   - Immediate attention for any vocalizations may promote language development.
   - The restatement can also correct speech in a nondirective manner.

5) **TARGET naturally occurring SOCIAL and PLAY SKILLS.**
   - Social skills:
     – This can include requesting, sharing, or taking turns.
     – Use praise to underline social interaction in your child's play.
     – Model the skill, and label your interactive behavior (e.g., when giving the crayon you are using to the child, say, "I would like to share my crayon with you.")
     – Teach without being directive or leading the play.
   - Play skills:
     – This can include using imaginative play with a doll or creating a story with characters.
     – Use praise to underline what you notice in the child's play.
     – Model plausible extension of your child's play behavior (e.g., if the child is pushing cars around, say, "Your cars are driving around getting ready for a race. Here's the starting line.")

6) **PRAISE your child as often as you can!**
   - Focus on "positive opposite" behaviors. For example, if your child usually takes toys from you without asking, praise any instance that he asks if he can play with a toy you are holding.

7) **AVOID commands or direct teaching of play.**
   - The short-term goal is to promote interactive play skills.
   - Interactive play skills are not about suggesting what the child should do.
   - If the child doesn't obey, the play can become unpleasant.

IF THE CHILD BECOMES UPSET DURING THE PLAY,
END THE PLAY CALMLY AND TRY AGAIN LATER!

Activity Sheet 5.5

Planning a Play Time

1. What sounds better, initiating play during structured play times or in more naturalistic situations?

_____

2. What seems like a realistic length of time to play together?

_____

3. Where should the play take place?

_____

4. How often will the play occur (daily, every couple of days)?

_____

5. Is there a certain time of the day that would work best to play with your child?

_____

6. What kind of toys or activities do you think might promote engagement in reciprocal play with your child?

_____

7. What play skills and/or social skills could be incorporated during the play?

_____

_____

Activity Sheet 5.6

Play Time Homework Sheet

Date	Time	Length of Practice	Activity	Specific Play/Social Skill Prompts	Problems or Questions

Activity Sheet 5.7

Catching Your Child Being Good

Activity/Time	Date	Date	Date	Date	Date	Date	Date

Reinforcers to Use: _____

Session Five Review

Catching Your Child Being Good

You can use social reinforcement, paired with tangible or material reinforcement if needed, during informal as well as formal interactions with your child. Whenever possible, use social reinforcement (high-five, "good job," "that was great the way you put away the toys") to acknowledge positive behaviors in everyday life. We call this "catching your child being good."

Play Skills

Another more formal way of reinforcing (i.e., promoting) appropriate behavior is to set up a structured play time with your child where you practice positive reinforcement skills.

Strategies to Encourage Joint Play

The goal of play time is to interact with your child with minimal direction of the child's behavior or play. To the extent possible, LET YOUR CHILD LEAD THE PLAY. As your child plays, you watch and appreciate what your child is doing. You also provide careful attention and social reinforcement. Here's a list of skills you can try out during play time:

1) OBSERVE your child in close proximity.
2) DESCRIBE what you are seeing after a brief period of observation.
3) IMITATE your child's play.
4) REFLECT what your child says—either by repeating or paraphrasing.
5) PROMOTE positive social or play skills with social reinforcement.
6) TAKE ADVANTAGE of ANY opportunity to praise your child's positive behavior.

Don't forget to label the behavior.

What to Do If Your Child Misbehaves

If your child is becoming agitated during the play, it's ok to play quietly for a moment without providing attention to the negative behaviors that emerge. If your child does not appear to be calming down, then quietly leave the play. Let the child know that play time is done and that you can play together again later in the day.

How to Set Up a Play Time

Some parents may want to take advantage of moments when the child is already playing with a toy or activity that he normally enjoys and is appropriate. You can also formalize the play time and let the child know that you play with him at a specific time each day.

Activity Sheet 6.1

Video Examples

Steps	Video #1	Video #2
1. Avoid eye contact; don't look at the child		
2. Do not touch the child; walk away if necessary		
3. Use a "neutral" facial expression; don't react		
4. Do not talk to the child or respond to him		
5. Make "ignoring" obvious, abrupt, and exaggerated		

Activity Sheet 6.2

Implementing Planned Ignoring at Home

1. What behavior do you want to decrease?	
2. What kind of ignoring will you use?	
3. What do you think will happen?	
4. What will you do if the behavior gets worse?	

Activity Sheet 6.3

Home Data Sheet

Behavior(s) to be ignored: _____

Type of ignoring to use: _____

Date	Time	Behavior	What Happened?

Session Six Review

Review of Consequences

A consequence is something that happens after the behavior. Consequences that are enjoyable increase the behavior. Consequences that are unpleasant decrease the behavior. Sometimes parents choose a consequence that is intended to stop their child's problematic behavior, but it makes the behavior worse instead of better. This is because the selected consequence actually reinforces the child's inappropriate behavior.

Planned Ignoring

Planned ignoring is a consequence that can be used to reduce attention-seeking behaviors. To use planned ignoring well, you must do the following:

- Avoid eye contact; don't look at the child.
- Do not touch the child; walk away if necessary.
- Use a "neutral" facial expression; don't react.
- Do not talk to the child or respond to him or her.
- Make sure that your ignoring is obvious, abrupt, and exaggerated—for example, turning away and folding your arms.

Potential Problems With Using Planned Ignoring

1. Behaviors that are ignored will often get worse before they get better.
2. Some behaviors cannot always be ignored.
3. Children can learn to be persistent. If you don't think that you can follow through with planned ignoring, "give in" immediately.
4. Planned ignoring can take a while to work.

Three Types of Planned Ignoring

1. *Ignore the Child and the Behavior* means paying no attention to the child or the child's behavior (e.g., temper tantrums).
2. *Ignore the Child but Not the Behavior* is used in response to dangerous or destructive behaviors. This involves using physical guidance or touch to prevent harm to the child, others, or property while otherwise ignoring the child.
3. *Ignore the Behavior but Not the Child* is used in response to repetitive and socially annoying behaviors. This involves responding to the child but continuing to ignore the repetitive or annoying behavior.

Compliance Training

Activity Sheet 7.1

Compliance Worksheet

COMPLIANCE COMMANDS: List 8 Requests Your Child Will Readily Follow

1. _____

2. _____

3. _____

4. _____

5. _____

6. _____

7. _____

8. _____

NONCOMPLIANCE COMMANDS: List 8 Requests Your Child Will Not Follow

1. _____

2. _____

3. _____

4. _____

5. _____

6. _____

7. _____

8. _____

Activity Sheet 7.2

Steps for Compliance Training in the Home

Step 1: Stand close to your child and get his attention.

Step 2: Tell your child what to do (don't ask!)
- State the command clearly so your child knows exactly what to do.
- State the command only once.

Step 3: At the same time, physically guide your child to complete the command.
- Once your child starts to comply, lessen physical guidance.

Step 4: As your child complies, provide immediate, specific praise.

Over time, reduce the amount of physical guidance you provide and give commands from an increasingly greater distance.

Activity Sheet 7.3

Video Examples

Steps	Video #1	Video #2	Video #3	Video #4	Video #5
Get child's attention					
Tell (don't ask) child what to do					
Provide physical guidance while giving request, even if child is resisting					
Praise child for compliance					

Activity Sheet 7.4

Homework Data Sheet

Compliance Commands List (Indicate if command was followed by circling Yes/No)

Command	Date	Date	Date	Date	Date	Date	Date
1.	YES NO	YES NO	YES NO	YES NO	YES NO	YES NO	YES NO
2.	YES NO	YES NO	YES NO	YES NO	YES NO	YES NO	YES NO
3.	YES NO	YES NO	YES NO	YES NO	YES NO	YES NO	YES NO

Additional Reinforcers Needed: _____

Noncompliance Commands List (Indicate if command was followed by circling Yes/No)

Command	Date	Date	Date	Date	Date	Date	Date
1.	YES NO	YES NO	YES NO	YES NO	YES NO	YES NO	YES NO
2.	YES NO	YES NO	YES NO	YES NO	YES NO	YES NO	YES NO
3.	YES NO	YES NO	YES NO	YES NO	YES NO	YES NO	YES NO

Additional Reinforcers Needed: _____

Comments: _____

Session Seven Review

Introduction to Compliance

Children don't comply with parent requests for a variety of reasons. Some children have difficulty paying attention and often don't even hear the instruction from the parent. Other children mean well, but once they start doing what they've been asked to do, they get distracted. Still other children are openly defiant. Noncompliant behavior may range from ignoring the parent request, to saying "no, no, no," to tantrums that vary in duration and severity. No matter the reason, noncompliance can become a habit that children learn when they are given commands and are permitted not to comply. Increasing compliance in children involves setting in place a new habit. We want your child to listen to your instructions and follow through on your commands the first time he or she hears them.

Four Steps for Compliance Training

Step 1: Stand close to your child and get his attention.

Step 2: Tell your child what to do (don't ask!).

Step 3: At the same time, physically guide your child to complete the command. Physical guidance involves providing gentle physical assistance to help a child comply with a command.

Step 4: As your child complies, provide immediate, specific praise.

Over time, reduce the amount of physical guidance you provide and give commands from an increasingly greater distance.

Using Compliance Training to Teach Your Child to "Stop"

Parents often tell their children to stop behaving in ways that are annoying, disruptive, or dangerous. Noncompliant behavior in children with ASD is complicated by the fact that they may not know what appropriate behaviors parents are expecting instead of the unacceptable behavior. The next time you find yourself telling your child to stop a behavior, practice compliance training. Walk over to your child, get his attention, and give an instruction that tells him what he should do. The key is to be explicit when giving the instruction, provide the necessary amount of guidance, and praise the child for complying.

Common Problems with Compliance Training

If a child becomes resistant or aggressive when physical guidance is provided, first work on commands that can easily and quickly be accomplished. If you think that social reinforcement will not be enough to promote compliance, the use of tangible reinforcers may be used in addition to social reinforcement.

Activity Sheet 8.1

<u>Case Example #1</u>

Tommy is a 5-year-old boy with a vocabulary of approximately 10 words. When his sister takes away one of his toys, he quickly becomes agitated and hits her until she gives back the toy.

What might Tommy be trying to communicate with his hitting?

_____

_____

What communication behaviors might be considered for Tommy to replace the hitting?

_____

_____

_____

How could you go about teaching this skill /behavior to Tommy?

_____

_____

_____

Case Example #2

Theresa is a 4-year-old girl who is extremely talkative. She chats about her interests and lets her parents know what she wants in general. However, at school she becomes very upset when a teacher asks her to leave the play area. Theresa will have a tantrum and refuse to leave the area.

What might Theresa be trying to communicate with her tantrum?

_____

_____

What communication behaviors might be considered to replace her noncompliance?

_____

_____

_____

How could you go about teaching this skill/behavior to Theresa?

_____

_____

_____

Activity Sheet 8.2

Your Child's Behavior to Change

_____

_____

Purpose or Function of That Behavior

_____

_____

Level of Your Child's Communication Skills (describe)

_____

_____

What communication behavior might be considered to be taught to replace your child's target behavior (manual sign, verbalization, picture, clap or other gesture, communication device)?

_____

_____

HOW TO GET STARTED

Outline steps to include one-on-one teaching and teaching in naturalistic setting (s). Also describe any additional supports (i.e., visuals, concrete symbols) that you feel may be supportive within the process.

_____

_____

_____

_____

_____

_____

Activity Sheet 8.3

Data Collection

Individual Teaching Opportunities

Situation, Date, and Time	No. of Teaching Attempts	No. of Times Successful	Prompts Needed

Naturalistic Teaching Opportunities (outside of one-on-one teaching)

Situation, Date, and Time	No. of Teaching Attempts	No. of Times Successful	Prompts Needed

Reflection: What went well? What would you do differently next time?

_____

_____

_____

_____

Session Eight Review

Introduction to Functional Communication Training

Functional communication training aims to replace the child's noncompliant and defiant behavior with a more appropriate way for communicating wants or needs, for example by using a sign, picture, or just "using your words." This new way of communicating will serve the same purpose as the problem behavior and be more "functional."

Before you begin teaching your child a new, alternative communication behavior to replace a problem behavior, however, always stop and think about the function of the inappropriate behavior. Indeed, the success of functional communication training depends on knowing what is driving the problem behavior.

Here are a few things to consider when you are trying to replace a challenging behavior with a more appropriate or functional way of communicating:

1. The replacement communication behavior **should work quickly** for the child. If you say "Use your words when you want a cookie," give the cookie when the child asks.
2. The replacement communication behavior **should work every time** for the child. This should extend to other adults who regularly interact with the child.
3. The replacement communication behavior **should require less effort** than the challenging behavior. Throwing a tantrum requires a lot of time and energy by the child! If a child can learn to hand a parent a picture or use a short phrase to get the same needs met, the more functional communication behavior requires much less effort.

The replacement behavior may take time and practice before it is regularly used in everyday situations. To promote the child's success, try to match the functional behavior with your child's developmental level.

Activity Sheet 9.1

1. What specific skills could I teach my child that might help with disruptive behaviors?

_____

_____

_____

_____

2. What skills would make my child more independent and not as reliant on me?

_____

_____

_____

_____

3. What skills does my child seem to be able to do most of the steps for but does not do, refuses to do, or finds frustrating?

_____

_____

_____

_____

4. What would my child be motivated to learn?

_____

_____

_____

_____

Activity Sheet 9.2

Task Analyzing a Skill

1. What skill would you like to teach? _____

2. Use Activity Sheet #3a to break down the skill into easy steps to learn.

3. On Activity Sheet #3a mark with a star the steps you need to teach your child.

4. What step will you start with? _____ Circle that step.

5. Circle which type of chaining will you use: BACKWARD FORWARD

6. What reinforcers do you want to give to reward your child's attempts?

   _____

   _____

   _____

   _____

7. During what naturally occurring times can you practice this skill?

   _____

   _____

   _____

   _____

8. During what structured times can you practice this skill?

   _____

   _____

   _____

   _____

Activity Sheet 9.3a

Homework Assignment

Skill to Teach: _____

List each step in the skill. For each date you practice, record the following:

  + = Completed independently;

InP = In progress, practiced but needs help;

 NI = Not introduced

Steps of Skill	Date	Date	Date	Date	Date	Date	Date
1.							
2.							
3.							
4.							
5.							
6.							
7.							
8.							

Activity Sheet 9.3b

Homework Assignment Example

Skill to Teach: Brushing Teeth

List each step in the skill. For each date you practice, record the following:

+ = Completed independently;
InP = In progress, practiced but needs help;
NI = Not introduced

Steps of Skill	Date 3/4	Date 3/5	Date 3/6	Date 3/7	Date 3/8	Date 3/9	Date 3/10
1. Unscrew toothpaste lid	+	+	+	+	+	+	+
2. Put toothpaste on brush	+	+	+	+	+	+	+
3. Rinse brush	InP	+	+	+	+	+	+
4. Brush bottom left	NI	InP	+	+	+	+	+
5. Brush bottom right	NI	NI	InP	InP	InP	+	+
6. Brush top right	NI	NI	NI	NI	NI	InP	+
7. Brush top left	NI	NI	NI	NI	NI	NI	InP
8. Rinse	NI	NI	NI	NI	NI	NI	NI

Session Nine Review

Children with ASD often need extra help in learning a new skill. This may require a systematic teaching plan. Here are some considerations that may help you select a new skill or behavior to target for teaching:

1. Which skill could I teach my child that might help reduce his disruptive behaviors (e.g., greater independence in getting dressed may reduce the daily struggle with getting dressed)?
2. Which skills would make my child more independent and less reliant on me?
3. Which skill does my child seem able to do but does not do completely, refuses to do, or finds frustrating?
4. What would my child be interested in learning?

Steps for Teaching a New Skill

1. First do a task analysis of the skill to break it down into its basic steps. Most skills are tasks that can be broken down into much smaller steps. This is referred to as a task analysis of a skill. A careful task analysis of the steps involved in mastering a skill is often essential before you can teach it.
2. Determine what steps your child can already do independently and what steps will need to be explicitly taught.
3. Choose where your starting place will be for teaching the skill and what kind of "chaining" you will use (backward chaining or forward chaining). Teaching a skill step by step is called chaining. This approach allows the child to focus on learning just that one step at a time. When using chaining, you continue to add steps one by one until the child is able to complete all of the steps in the task analysis. The next thing to consider is the order to teach the steps. For example, you can use forward chaining, where you start by teaching the very first step in the task analysis and build up from there, or you can use backward chaining, where you start with the very last step in the task analysis and work backward.
4. Start by teaching one particular step of the chain at a time. Once the child has mastered a particular step in the task analysis, move onto the next step.
5. Complete all other steps in the task that your child has not yet mastered.
6. Provide reinforcement for all attempts your child makes to complete that step. As you increase the number of steps that the child needs to complete independently, you can praise your child as he completes each step, but hold off on providing a big reinforcer until those steps are completed.

Activity Sheet 10.1a

1. What skill would you like to teach? _____

2. List on Activity Sheet #1b each step in the skill.

3. On Activity Sheet #1b mark with a star the steps you need to teach your child.

4. What step will you start with? _____   Circle that step.

5. Circle which type of chaining you will use: BACKWARD   FORWARD

6. What reinforcers do you want to give to reward your child's attempts?

   _____

   _____

7. What types of prompts will you use for each step?

   _____

   _____

8. During what naturally occurring times can you practice this skill?

   _____

   _____

9. During what structured times can you practice this skill?

   _____

   _____

Activity Sheet 10.1b

Response Prompt Homework Assignment

For each date you practice, record the following:

Skill Mastery: **+** = Completed independently
InP = In progress, practiced but needs help
NI = Not introduced

Prompts Used: **Mo** = Modeled   **Vis** = Visual Prompt   **Ver** = Verbal Prompt
Ges = Gestural Prompt **Phy** = Physical Prompt **PP** = Partial Physical Prompt

Step	Prompts	Date	Date	Date	Date	Date	Date	Date
1.								
2.								
3.								
4.								
5.								
6.								
7.								
8.								
9.								
10.								

Comments or issues when teaching skill:

Activity Sheet 10.2a

Stimulus Prompt Homework Assignment

1. What skill would you like to teach? _____

2. Will you use "fading in" or "fading out" to teach this skill? _____

3. What stimulus prompts do you want to start with? _____

4. How will the stimulus prompts change over time? _____

5. What reinforcers to you want to give to reward your child's attempts?

   _____

6. What types of prompts can you use for each step?

   _____

   _____

   _____

7. During what naturally occurring times can you practice this skill?

   _____

   _____

   _____

8. During what structured times can you practice this skill?

   _____

   _____

   _____

Activity Sheet 10.2b

Stimulus Prompt Homework Assignment Example

For each date you practice, record the following:

Skill Mastery: + = Completed independently
    InP = In progress, practiced but needs help
    NI = Not introduced

Prompts Used: **Mo** = Modeled   **Vis** = Visual Prompt   **Ver** = Verbal Prompt
    Ges = Gestural Prompt   **Phy** = Physical Prompt   **PP** = Partial Physical Prompt

Step	Prompts	Date 3/6	Date 3/7	Date 3/8	Date 3/9	Date 3/10	Date 3/11	Date 3/12
1. Sort 3 red and 3 green blocks	Phy, Ver	InP	+	+	+	+	+	+
2. Sort 5 red and 5 green blocks	Phy, Ver		InP	InP	+	+	+	+
3. Sort 5 red, 5 green, 1 yellow block	Phy, Ver				InP	+	+	+
4. Sort 5 red, 5 green, 3 yellow blocks	Phy, Ver					InP	+	+
5. Sort 5 red, 5 green, 5 yellow blocks	Phy, Ver						InP	+
6.								
7.								
8.								
9.								
10.								

Activity Sheet 10.2c

Stimulus Prompt Homework Assignment

For each date you practice, record the following:

Skill Mastery: + = Completed independently
    InP = In progress, practiced but needs help
    NI = Not introduced

Prompts Used: **Mo** = Modeled   **Vis** = Visual Prompt   **Ver** = Verbal Prompt
    Ges = Gestural Prompt   **Phy** = Physical Prompt   **PP** = Partial Physical Prompt

Step	Prompts	Date	Date	Date	Date	Date	Date	Date	Date
1.									
2.									
3.									
4.									
5.									
6.									
7.									
8.									
9.									
10.									

Comments or issues when teaching skill:

Activity Sheet 10.3a

Time Delay Homework Assignment

1. What skill would you like to teach? _____

2. How will you use a time delay when teaching this skill?

   _____

   _____

3. How will you measure the time delay? (e.g., count in head, egg timer)

   _____

   _____

4. How will the stimulus prompts change over time?

   _____

   _____

5. What types of prompts can you use for each step?

   _____

   _____

6. During what naturally occurring times can you practice this skill?

   _____

   _____

7. During what structured times can you practice this skill?

   _____

   _____

Activity Sheet 10.3b

Time Delay Homework Assignment Example

For each date you practice, record the following:

Skill Mastery:

       + = Completed independently

   InP = In progress; practiced but needs help

Step	Date 3/4	Date 3/5	Date 3/6	Date 3/7	Date 3/8	Date 3/9	Date 3/10	Date 3/11
1. Name color Red	InP	+	+	+	+	+	+	+
2. Name color Blue		InP	InP	InP	+	+	+	+
3. Name color Purple					InP	+	+	+
4. Name color Green						InP	InP	+
5.								
6.								
7.								
8.								

Comments or issues when teaching skill:

Activity Sheet 10.3c

Time Delay Homework Assignment

For each date you practice, record the following:

Skill Mastery:

          + = Completed independently

         InP = In progress; practiced but needs help

Step	Date	Date	Date	Date	Date	Date	Date	Date
1.								
2.								
3.								
4.								
5.								
6.								
7.								
8.								

Comments or issues when teaching skill:

Session Ten Review

Introduction to Prompting

When learning a new skill, we all need some help. There are many ways to help children learn new skills and patterns of behavior. Prompting is one way to help your child learn and incorporate new skills while you are giving a direction at the same time.

Different Types of Prompting

There are several types of prompts that can be used to teach your child a new skill:

1. *Modeling* is when you show your child what you want him to do so that he can learn the skill by observing and then imitating you.
2. *Verbal Prompts* are things that you **SAY** to remind your child what you want him to do. The reminder is a hint that may help your child to incorporate the new skill. Another type of verbal prompt is deliberate stress on a particular word such as "hand me the RED car."
3. *Visual Prompts* are things that your child can **SEE** that show him what you want him to do. Gestures are the most common kind of visual prompt we use. Types of visual prompts that we have already reviewed include visual schedules, picture prompts, and timers. Timers provide a visual cue to signal when an activity is ending or a transition needs to occur.
4. *Physical Prompts* involve the use of physical guidance with your hands or body to help your child **DO** a task. The level of physical guidance depends on how much assistance is needed. For example, a full physical prompt may be needed when your child is not familiar with the skill you are trying to impart and so needs a lot of assistance going through the motions to carry out the task. A partial physical prompt, such as a hand on a shoulder, is used when your child has some familiarity with the task.

Stimulus Prompts and Stimulus Fading

So far, we have focused on "response prompts." These are prompts from another person designed to elicit a certain response from the child. Sometimes you might use "stimulus prompts," in which an object or stimulus is used to prompt the desired response from the child.

Time Delay Procedure

Another useful prompting technique is the time delay procedure. In this approach, the prompt is presented to the child only after a certain amount of time has passed and the child has not given the correct response.

Summary

When teaching skills, use only the prompting that is needed to promote a successful response. Use several types of prompts when introducing a new skill. Then gradually fade your prompts over time as your child masters the skill.

Activity Sheet 11.1

Progress Review

1. What specific improvements in challenging behaviors have you seen in your child?

   _____

   _____

2. What new skills has your child learned? _____

   _____

3. How have these changes improved daily life and your family? _____

   _____

Is It Time for Maintenance?

1. What behavior(s) are you hoping to maintain over time? _____

   _____

2. What would be a realistic and acceptable level for this behavior? _____

   _____

3. Do you feel that this behavior is at an acceptable level? _____

What to Generalize

1. What new behaviors has your child learned to do across settings (e.g., school, home, restaurant, grocery store)? _____

   _____

2. Are there any new behaviors that your child still needs to learn to do across settings? _____

   _____

3. What new behaviors has your child learned to when conditions vary? _____

   _____

4. Are there any new behaviors that your child needs help learning to do across varying conditions?

   _____

   _____

Activity Sheet 11.2

Maintenance Tips

1. Continued reinforcement is important in maintaining a behavior. Sometimes a new behavior will not continue when it is no longer reinforced.

2. Using a delayed (after a certain period of time) or intermittent (given only some of the time) reinforcement schedule, you can fade reinforcement of the skill to a more realistic level.

Generalization Tips

1. New skills are more likely to be generalized if they are reinforced across different settings.

2. It is helpful to use reinforcers that naturally occur in different settings.

3. If a situation is too different from the one the skill was learned in, sometimes the new skill will not generalize to the new situation.

4. Make sure a problematic behavior is not being reinforced in situations outside of the home.

Activity Sheet 11.3a

Video Vignettes

Video #1 –Sorting Legos

What ideas would you suggest in order to promote maintenance and generalization of this skill?

Maintenance Suggestions:

1. _____

2. _____

Generalization Suggestions:

1. _____

2. _____

Video #2 – Help Card

What ideas would you suggest in order to promote maintenance and generalization of this skill?

Maintenance Suggestions:

1. _____

2. _____

Generalization Suggestions:

1. _____

2. _____

Activity Sheet 11.3b

Written Vignettes

Example #1

Timothy is consistently using the toilet at home, for which he is reinforced by being allowed to watch a few minutes of his favorite video. What steps might we take next to be sure he uses the toilet in other places?

Maintenance Suggestions:

1. _____

2. _____

Generalization Suggestions:

1. _____

2. _____

Example #2

Toby's aggression toward adults has decreased from 15 times a day to several days with no aggression. Toby is reward every 5 minutes for "keeping his hands to himself." He has also been taught to ask for help when he is frustrated by a task. What steps would you take to make sure his aggression remains minimal and he uses his verbal skills to request help?

Maintenance Suggestions:

1. _____

2. _____

Generalization Suggestions:

1. _____

2. _____

Activity Sheet 11.4

Homework

MAINTENANCE

Target Behavior(s):

1. For behaviors that are at an appropriate level, how are they currently being rewarded?

_____

_____

_____

2. How can this reinforcement system be maintained over time?

_____

_____

_____

GENERALIZATION

Target Behavior(s):

1. How can this skill or behavior be generalized to other places?

_____

_____

_____

2. How can this behavior be reinforced in other situations?

_____

_____

_____

Session Eleven Review

The Concept of Maintenance

As new positive behaviors begin to take hold, it is time to think about how they can be continued into the future. We call this maintenance. We all want the newly acquired positive behaviors to last.

The Concept of Generalization

We also want to increase the likelihood that the positive behaviors occur in different settings and when conditions vary, such as with different types of materials and with a variety of people. We call this generalization. It refers to the child's successful transfer of positive behavior to situations other than those in which training takes place.

Tips to Promote Skill Maintenance

1. Continued reinforcement is essential to maintain positive behavior.
2. Fade reinforcement of the new behavior over time so that the behavior has a life of its own. For example, you might move from reinforcing a behavior every time to reinforcing a behavior every third or fifth time; this would be an example of intermittent reinforcement. Parents may also use delayed reinforcement in which reinforcement is not immediate but given after a gradually increasing period of time.

Tips to Promote Generalization

1. New skills are more likely to generalize if they are reinforced across different settings.
2. Try to use reinforcers that naturally occur in different settings—for example, letting the child watch a favorite DVD at home and listen to a favorite CD in the car.
3. If new situations are too different from the original situation, the new skill may not generalize without new training.
4. Make sure that the problem behavior is not being reinforced in situations outside of the home.

About the Authors

Karen Bearss, PhD, is Assistant Professor in the Department of Psychiatry and Behavioral Sciences at the University of Washington. She directs the RUBI clinic at the Seattle Children's Autism Center.

Cynthia R. Johnson, PhD, is the Director of the Cleveland Clinic Center for Autism in Cleveland Ohio and faculty at the Lerner College of Medicine, Case Western Reserve University.

Benjamin L. Handen, PhD, is Professor of Psychiatry and Pediatrics at the University of Pittsburgh School of Medicine and Director of Research and Clinical Services at the Center for Autism and Developmental Disorders at Western Psychiatric Institute and Clinic.

Eric Butter, PhD, is a pediatric psychologist, Associate Professor of Pediatrics and Psychology at the Ohio State University, and Chief of Psychology at Nationwide Children's Hospital in Columbus, Ohio.

Luc Lecavalier, PhD, is a clinical psychologist and Professor of Psychology and Psychiatry at the Ohio State University.

Tristram Smith, PhD, is a licensed psychologist, board-certified behavior analyst and Haggerty-Friedman Professor of Developmental/Behavioral Pediatric Research at the University of Rochester Medical Center.

Lawrence Scahill, MSN, PhD, is Professor of Pediatrics at the Emory University School of Medicine and Director of Clinical Trials at the Marcus Autism Center in Atlanta.